Also by Cassie Premo Steele

Anthology:
*Moon Days*
Fiction:
*Shamrock and Lotus*
Nonfiction:
*We Heal from Memory*
*My Peace*
*Easyhard*
Poetry:
*Ruin*
*This is how honey runs (print)*
*This is how honey runs (audio with music)*

# THE POMEGRANATE PAPERS

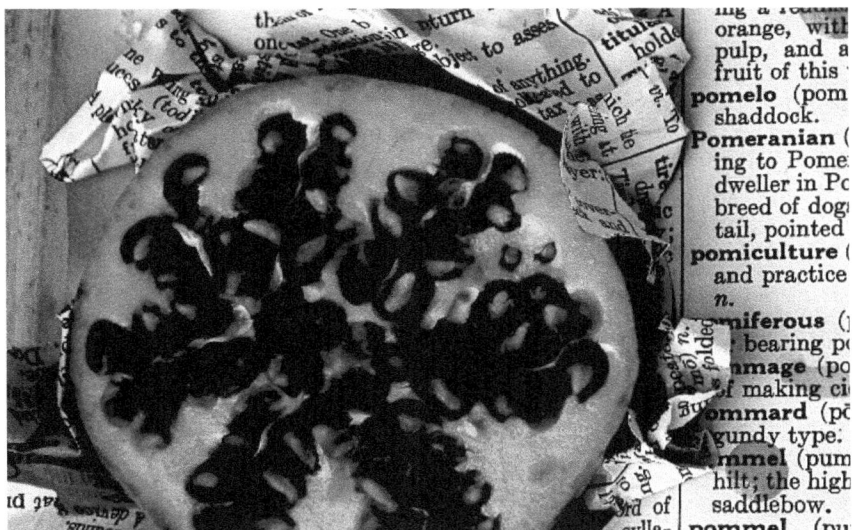

## CASSIE PREMO STEELE

ISBN 978-1-936373-26-0

Published in the United States by Unbound Content, LLC, Englewood, NJ.
Cover art: ©2012, by Jeff Smyers
Author photo: ©2011, by Sofia Tata, www.sofiatata.com

THE POMEGRANATE PAPERS

First edition 2012

unbound CONTENT

For Meili
and Laura
and Lily
with love and gratitude
for what we have created
together

# TABLE OF CONTENTS

## To Survive and Give Birth, and Be the Midwife
By Cassie Premo Steele

This spring, on the day this volume is published, I will turn forty-five. It is a nice, solid number. A number in the center of midlife. Long ago, I wrote the poem, "Persephone," which is the central poem that developed into this book. I was a young wife, still mostly defined by my role as a daughter, when I wrote this. And I was also a new stepmother. My stepdaughter was nine years old. So marriage initiated me into mothering. The mothering of a daughter.

The story of Demeter and Persephone is well-known. It is the story all mothers and daughters must live through as the daughter grows and learns to be her own woman.

What is less well remembered is that Persephone becomes a mother in the underworld. She bears a son with the god of the underworld, and it is mothering itself, in addition to the pomegranate seeds that she eats, that compels her cyclic return to her husband and son as she negotiates her life between her alliances with her mother and her new family.

For the mother, the separation entails loss, pain and mourning, as she comes to terms with the lack of her own power over her daughter and the consequences of her own aging. It is a wise old woman who counsels the mother at this time, telling her to "spill" the tears and honey, to let her emotions flow into something sweet of her own making.

I have felt this pain and loss at the inevitable growth and individuation of my children, as well. I see how their independence demands a separation from me. It is the necessary —and poetic—paradox of mothering well.

For the daughter, the pain is the mirror face of disappointment that the mother cannot protect her from all harm and that she must learn to live with the circumstances of her life—those that have been thrust upon her and those that have been chosen.

I have seen my own face in this mirror, too, as I have learned to embrace the mothering I received—some of it very similar to the way my mother mothered me (the laugh! the dance!) —and some of it very different. The garden. The writing. Learning to accept it all.

Each spring we celebrate the return of Persephone to her mother Demeter—and the reunion between mother and daughter as the earth blossoms back to life after a long, hard winter. The seasonal nature of the story reveals the recurring way in which we can accomplish the re-integration of the mother within us as daughters, the daughter within us as mothers.

As these poems go out from me, I will be reminded that all of our creations are like children who must one day leave. And on the day that I get on the first plane for my book tour, I will remember that we women can be all three of the parts in this story over the course of our lives.

There are times we can be the mother, the one who holds and cares for the house during the daughter's growth and going away and return. We can be the wise woman, the one who counsels our friends and ourselves to hold on during the hardest seasons. And we can once again be the daughter, as we let ourselves leave so we can grow and become who we are as fully filled, blossoming and creative women.

## Here is the woman awakening

Here is the woman awakening
even as she dreams.
Here is the leap she is taking
where the sky becomes her beams.
She joins the stillness of creation
when she pauses at midflight.
She wins the praise and adoration
of all she had to fight.
Here is the woman waiting,
here is her future in the dark.
Here is the discovery she is making,
the dirt she tills at daybreak
where something sleeping wants to start.

## Conception

We swam back first,
between and within,
the night we made love
and welcomed you,
your first fold and swim.

It was Easter, when all things rise again.
The moon was rising,
and the seedlings in the flower bed,
and the sturdy stalks of iris outside our window.

The stars came slowly
and beckoned me outside,
after, while your father slept.
I whispered by the light
of the night that you were
welcome, and I know now
that you heard me, clear.

Welcome, dear.
Welcome, dear.

## Your First Folding

My water is a wonder to you,
as you begin in the night,
under cover of love and starlight.

You divide in on yourself,
fold over like hands
in prayer or eyes
in the sun, doubling
to make yourself one.

Water curves, too,
makes elbows and knees
of the earth,
moves what needs
to be planted,
delivers what needs
to give birth.

## My Body

I.
Was a measure,
a stick a bit
too short.
I claimed
and tamed
her territories.
I made her mine
to birth
or abort.

II.
She became
a subject when
you entered.
She took back
her sovereign
reign.
Reclaimed
her flag,
her name.

III.
Ever after
you will be known
as liberator.
The activist
who reignited
faith, and flame.
I burn
with whole
movements.

IV.
I am one
with spider,
rose and river.
I spill over
edges,
wild and tame.
I am
a pregnant
woman,
clear and sane.

## The fires

The fires I fought with moons ago
have dwindled to mere cinders now.
I ran and stomped from engine-rooms,
said goodbye to rubber boots
and red shield hats and gloves.
My papers used to burn with certainty.
I touched them daily with my water hose, my pen.
Until a larger burn on the horizon
entered me, and life began within.
I blaze now, an eight-week star
in me, growing hot and red, an ember
fed by my warm red blood, my bed.
I dance across the air, canyons
in each step. I climb mountains
sitting still. I do not worry over
what I have left. The fires of word
will burn again, and poetry will dance—
a fine duet of maternity, a ballet
of breast and womb and chance.

## Dreamsongs

When lying deep inside our mother's wombs
we first learned to hear voices
from beyond the skin, our tombs,

the otherworldly noises that sang
to us in foreign tongues. In the dark
we did not know when we were dreaming.

So we learned to listen to the singing
and to see what we were seeing
with other eyes—our ears.

We danced, too, to our dreamsongs,
wiggling wet limbs and hairy faces,
and with this movement

our mothers dreamt of us as we
were dreaming of this world,
a world of sound and light

that makes us more than visible,
where dreams are more than possible,
when we sing of every living thing in us.

## On the verge

A mango long, you swim
sweetly in waters we share
through our tongues, your body is
done, save for growing.
You have hair, a downy skin
you feel things in,
the first sense, and always
the most intimate.
I have heard your heart,
tuned you in like a radio
at sunset, through static
and tipping earth.
You came in like a wave,
rushing the dark walls
of my cave. I can smell
you already, in my water,
they say I will know you
by this when you arrive.
They are wrong. I will know
you in the way a blind man
sees, a tree talks, and
the moon never leaves.
I am on the verge of mother,
and this is how I see.

## The voice of my husband

The voice of my husband haunts me, long distance,
in the wind on the shore, with him on dry land,
and our weathers converge in a storm. History
lies between us now, as we wait in the rain for the dawn.

Nothing will be the same. We brace in this hurricane,
trying to talk across crackling wires, our absence
an extended goodbye to ourselves, as one
or a pair, we know we are about to disappear.

The memory of our lovemaking, failed over fear,
lingers in the air over miles. And the voice
of my husband, what drew me to him,
compelled me like an affair, cuts through the distance.

We have nothing to worry about, he says.
And I believe him.

## The Wait

In the center of daylight I dig
beneath the earth, lying low
and dark, the drip a metronome
of nature's time. Here I wait
for wet and blood, the flood that comes
from where we came. The name
of life is waiting, and the earth
knows this. She waits for seasons,
waits for rain, waits for growth
and death and shedding, waits
even when she waits in vain.
What patience we could learn:
to know that each day holds behind
it night, to know each moment
leans from itself to turn, to know
that we are never late, as we unfurl
in the green and slow of fern.

## The moment of labor

You hold a white dove in your hand
as the leaves fall around you, delicate,
and your eyes, the burning hazel
in the trees, search for me, intimate,
the kind of open that comes from cracking
shells to reveal the inside flesh,
the meaty nut that must be eaten.

And I, on the other side of the window,
of the world, pretend to know the wind
that surrounds you now, in late autumn.
You wait—for your child to be born,
for your father to die again, as he does
each year, when the night is long
and all the leaves have fallen.

You cannot see me clearly on the inside,
in the dusk. You wonder at the gourd I carry,
the great water, the strong husk. I am a pumpkin
you cannot cut. You must wait
for my burst that signals the stepping
into your father's place. To be bare
like this, it is the hardest trial for a man.

And then, a noise—the splitting of the glass
from its frame—and my voice—calling—
It's time—and you are once again
in motion, no less frightened
but at least not standing still, as you move
to meet me at the door, as your footsteps
take you back to what you almost missed.

## Walking on the Backs of Whales

The night you were born I dreamt
I saw whales in the ocean, large humps
of backs rising out of the sea, grey
like your hands, and lingering there,
in the air, skin full of urchins and
moss. The sight was wondrous, like
your eyes, the first time you looked
at us, into the blue of me, the hazel
of your father, your gaze a miraculous
mix of us both. And when I was done,
with the whales and your birthing,
I began to walk back to the land,
and the water was shallow, the pain
was not bad, I was still amazed
at what I had seen, and I realized
I'd been walking on the backs of whales
the whole time. What I'd taken for earth
was the wet of their bodies, hovering firm
beneath the surface of water, providing
a path over ocean, allowing me to meet you
half way, between that world and this,
taking me gently back home to the shore
where I never before had been.

## In the image of me

In the image of me,
red and brown and bleeding,
the world was made—
not from word, so righteous,
not from breath, so dry,
not from light, so blinding,
not from air, so high—
but shy and wet
and dark and deep
came the world—
crying, crawling,
sweet-smelling
of mud and muck—
the world arrived in moans and sighs
from between my two strong thighs.

## The first moment

You hold her in your bony arms
and her blue eyes crackle at your voice,
the voice I fell in love with, the voice
you gave in love to me. As you give
her to me now, as you have been giving
all your life. This is what it means
to be a man: to give all you can,
in voice and body, heart and hand.
You gave her to me nine months ago,
a gift from your sea, and though
at times it seemed to me that you
departed for another shore, I know
now, as I hold her in my arms,
that you were there all along,
in her, in me, and will be, still,
after we are gone. We will be, still,
in her, your gift from my body,
long after both of us are gone.

## What a mother does

She births. Before the earth
bursts whole and yellow,
the egg cracks, white
and tight. She knows
that life is made of spillage,
that love blooms in light.

She feeds. Changing
her flesh to food daily,
she makes the miracle
possible within herself.
She is a double fountain,
a place to lay our mouth.

She loves. Like fierce
creatures that hide away,
lion, jaguar, fox, and hawk,
she tracks down prey
to feed her young, enjoys
the chase, the kill,
the maw of every day.

She sings. In fingers,
eyelids, silent things,
a song vibrates from
her body, a hymn of remembering
all that lives, her tune
the source of all that is.

## The truth is I am afraid

to leave you even for one breath. I want to suck and pull each gasp of air from you to keep you living. I am afraid if I am gone you will be too, and this branch that bears us both will break and pull you underground. I am afraid I have made you, whole, myself, and if I forget you will disappear, like the flower you neglect to pick that wilts and withers. I am afraid that if I do not hear your every cry, you will go voiceless, hard and silent. I am afraid that this fire that burns in me is your only furnace, and winter is coming, and I cannot stop working, or you will go out. I am afraid that my smell is what brings you back to me daily, after the drop and sink of sleep. I am afraid that I cannot feel complete again if you are not near, that I have become a cross and you are my other beam. I am afraid too that it is my fear that is killing you, slowly leaking the life from you, daily, that like a balloon you are deflating, or else one day, you will unexpectedly pop.

## What I cannot tell you

is how your touch arrived with loss, how, looking at you, I had to look away from your father, and myself, and how we were never the same again. How your eyes became my focus, not his, not mine for him, how we were strangers to each other, connected only by the ribbon of your skin. I cannot tell you that nothing was as important, not my writing, not my politics, not my sex. I wanted to lose myself in you, abandon everything, be where you were, and live only through you, through who you were becoming. But I cannot tell you this. I will pretend that the love between us, your father and I, is as strong as ever, that we have grown in our love for each other because of you, and that it is better, but different, all the things that people say. And I will tell you that my writing did not change, except to get better, I was more in touch with my emotions, felt a sympathy with other mothers, all the things that women writers say. And I will tell you that I grew too, became a different person, and this part will be true. I became the kind of person who can tell you lies and do it out of love, do it because the love I feel for you has changed everything.

## The first sea

I imagined you before you were born
as a water creature, but the mind
of a mother cannot hold the depths
of what gifts will come. How could I
have known how much you would love
the land, want to walk with me on it
after swimming for such a short time
in the flesh of my body? You cry,
the crash of the cold on your toes too much,
so I take you back to the edge of land
where the trees began, and your tears
mix with the salt and sand in my milk.
You drink it in, the love of this world,
as you begin to turn away from
your mother, as we all do, cry
for where we came from, even
as we walk away and say goodbye.

## Spring, again

The buds are forming on the apple trees
again, and we are coming to the blossom,
to the anniversary of your conception.
You are no guppy now, no longer swim
in my blind sea but skim spring
puddles with your own toes,
tapping out the sounds of rain.
I fear I have lost you already, the part
of you that was a part of me,
and this is what I'm mourning.
I long again for summer, the heavy hard
sweat of you, and then the fall, the
pungent pickled weight of you,
and then the winter, the fragrant freeze
of your arrival. Not spring.
Not the waiting, not the wanting,
not the life without you in it,
not desire coming from my lonely
lovely self. In spring we meet as
separate singers, each a rhythm, each a
part. The song we sing is my
lament, your celebration, as it is
for ever after: your happiness
leaves a tiny worm that feeds
upon the apple of my heart.

## Nine Months

You have been in this world
as long as you were in the world of my body.
Your hair, no longer matted the dark
color of water, waves to the wind
in morning. Your eyes, no longer
the deep blue of rainstorms, leave
behind them beams of sunlight
in the afternoon. Your hands,
in evening, no longer clutch
my breast, but tightly fisted
hug your own body, tug an ear,
hold yourself as you sail
into the nighttime ocean.
I am still in that other world,
more than you, and may be, still,
for ever after: I feel your feet kick
within me, I caress your head
beneath my sternum, I breathe
into my belly to see how far
my skin can still expand.
I could still take you into me,
if you need it, could shelter
your whole body, let you grow in me,
keep you safe from wind and sun and ocean,
let you sleep an endless night.

## Weaned

My nipples are shell pink again,
not the dirt red clay you lived
upon, the first sign that heralded
your arrival in me, the change
in color of a woman holding
a woman inside herself.
And now you move from my shore
once again, hold your bottle like a trumpet
announcing your departure away from me,
as my breasts recede and your vision
sharpens and you sail out,
far from the edge of my body's horizon,
leaving me feeling the chill of the coming
winter's season, for the first time in three years.

## I looked through the window

I looked through when I was waiting for you, and it was morning and you were gone to school when I heard the news that the head of your school has lost her baby. Lost? I thought, like I lost your shoe that I'd bought only the day before, and then I understood but I did not want to understand that he had never been born, the cord wrapped around his neck, and I wondered how they got him out, if they cut her open and if it's still called being born when you arrive here dead. I was thinking these awful thoughts so that I wouldn't imagine you as the baby, but it didn't work, and then I sobbed to think I might never have known you, the you who is already, in not even a year, a person in the world. To think you might have turned back and I would not even know what I was missing. Stupid. We are so stupid and cruel to let each minute pass that we are not indescribably grateful. So I cling, with the leaves changing, a little tighter to your skin, and admit that even if you were to slip from my hands this moment, I would still be grateful that you decided to come at all.

## Days of the Dead

I lay out plates of food for the dead
and circle their pictures there, to welcome
back spirits in this cold November air.
I show you your relations, and you wave
like you've seen them before, and I ask you
how they are doing, is my uncle
still drinking, is that one still crying,
does this one still like being a nun?
You smile at me, silly, as if to say how human
I am, as if you cannot believe that I
do not know that we are more
than all this, once we are dead.
I pause, shake my head,
try to imagine an alcoholic without his habit,
a nun without hers, a depressed woman
happy and away from her bed.
And then I see that what would remain
would be the mystery that makes people
love a baby, so full of hunger, dying to be fed,
our link back to the beginning, the needful
beat of being that goes on going
long after we all are dead.

## Moving Out

The first snow of the season,
just a few flakes, begins as we fill
our cars with clothes and kitchen things
to take them to the new house.

You are home, with daddy,
and I am helping my best friend
leave her husband, advising
her to sell what she no longer
needs, to start over fresh.

She asks me what I have
that I can give her: a colander,
a corkscrew, a waffle iron,
a cappuccino maker. All duplicate,
in drawers and cabinets at the house.

Our house, I think, holds you
in it, and so much extra,
so much to spare, I realize
as I drive across the river,
careful not to jostle the piles
of suits and wine glasses and the
wedding dress in the back seat.

As hard as it's been this year,
it's never been this hard,
I've never really even been close
to packing our lives away.

By the time I come home,
it is snowing for real,
and I join you on the floor
by your daddy, and we watch
the snow moving down from the sky
and hold you between us
and vow it will always be this way.

Early that evening you take
your first steps, three quiet
white footfalls that show
you are moving out, too.

And we cheer and we shout,
staying right where we are
so you will have something
to push off from and a goal
to work for, something unmelting
in the middle of moving day.

## Birthday

While the world prepares for Christmas,
the birth of another woman's son,
I notice the snow globe under our tree
is broken, the morning you turn one.

I wonder, worry—how I have worried
this year!—at the omen, then take out
the photo of our family at noon, and turn
it away from the crack, so that it is hidden,
invisible except from the back.

I have learned to do this as a mother,
find buttons that almost match,
buy shoes to replace those you've lost,
turn snow globes and do mountains of wash.

Nothing is as clean as you were that morning,
covered in white and glossy and wet.
I touched your temple, so light, with my finger,
rubbed the cream of your skin into my thumb,
felt such wonder at what I had done.

Today you will laugh and wave to balloons,
and tonight you will say, for the first time, "moon."
But for now you are sleeping, an afternoon nap
to prepare for the party, and the house is quiet,
and I can pretend, breathing hard and filling my belly
that you are still in me, a silent fish in my inner stream,
and all is still possible, and you have not left me,
and today I have nothing to do but dream.

## Birth Day

Write your self daily this year and
dance to each grin of your daughter.
Be in each moment like water.

Let desire rule your body, as
the ocean swells its tide in you.
Learn to grow through the currents.

You are a mother now, but
you are still a woman, so still
sleep long enough to dream.

Keep your fire alive, even as you tend to others.
Let them play their part. Each sacrifice is holy,
but only if it leads to a strong and happy heart.

## What a Wife Knows of Bones

I begin with the ridge of your foot, a fan
of sparrow feathers, so light, they sprout brown flight
while you sleep. The sky is your whole calf, the air
that rubs against me in the dark, that holds the memory
of the wooden bat cracking to make you run.
I reach your thigh, secure in its blankets of flesh,
the old woman who tells you to rest,
it's alright, after so many years, to sit down.
I caress her wavy grey hair and wander up the hip,
that shield, what you carry, what worries you
even when you dance. Turn you over, trace your spine,
the bricks of your fortress, what stands in the middle
of a traveling life. Each piece is a lattice that geraniums poke through.
And your ribs, glorious spoons scoop against me,
scrape up what is frozen like strawberry ice.
You pull back and there are wings from your neck
that spread open like a cross or the beginning of an embrace.
Your shoulders, silver goblets you dip your head into
when you hear Beethoven or the sound of your daughter's voice.
Your arms are the two pairs of drumsticks your father left you,
what he played in the basement and embedded
within you by what you remember was the rhythm of his eyes.
Your fingers, each a toddler in a blue colored schoolroom.
One squats at the knees and all the rest begin to laugh.
You wake, touch your face, that thin cover of what remains
of all of us after we are gone. The morning sun inches further
across our bed to your pillow. Another day of our marriage moves along.

## A Woman in Her Thirties

A woman in her thirties is a book
half open. Her arms are the up-
facing pages. They say, hug me
or shut. The leaves of her life
fold under her face, layers of snake
skin she has shed. Each tells
a story of a different self—completely
separate. She remembers who she was
as little as she knows who she will be.
Both are vague characters in her dreams.
She goes over and over the words
in front of her, looking for a clue
to duration. Sometimes she imagines
she has written this book.
Then her spine crackles with life.
Most days she admits that the author
is another, who has peeled back the covers,
inserted letters, cut out some parts with a knife.

## Memory

Years before your birth, I walked
on rocks, burnt black and bathed
in summer rain, still steaming.
I was alone. I had left your father
that summer, still dug in drought,
and drove across this land, my home.
I was searching for the poetry
that would be me. I found it
in the rocks, sketched hard by bone,
family pictures that lasted over
a thousand years. Hand, face, cat,
moon: what we remember of each other,
what I brought you here to see,
what I will never forget, will keep
giving you long after my memory.

## Mother Tongue

In a handmade book of cream colored paper
and a cover of blue and green, I will write your words
from the beginning.

I will start with Nana, your first word for the food
you eat and my mother, where we all come from
and where we will one day be.

I will record what you love and what you see—
bear, bunny, doll and ball—what you miss and call for
in the night—

Dada, your father, Wawa, your sister, and
Waawawa, your word for music
and singing and dance.

And me, I will put down my names—Mama, Mommy,
and Mom, I will be all of these women,
let you speak of me in many ways.

I will not erase it, I will not look away, and together
our tongues will take us back to the beginning,
to the food we eat, and our mother, where we
all come from, and where we will one day be.

## House Pleasures

In the middle of the day she thinks
of him out there talking in hallways
filled with people rushing to ringing
phones, and she gathers, in quiet,
the worn towels from the wash
and takes them to the middle
of the living room, where they have
made love and she has vacuumed
and toys have been. She lays them out,
soft and skin-like, all over the floor,
and smiles, placing them large like
a big patchwork quilt—the yellow
wash cloth and the blue bath towel,
the white, the green, the brown,
another blue. Together they are all
the quilts that women have ever made,
they take up so much space,
she must move newspapers and
his shoes in order to make room.
And when it is done, she sits
on the edge like on the edge
of a new lover's bed and looks
out across and wants to get
to the other side, wants to touch
every spot, feel its warmth and depth,
let its color cover her skin, so
she lays her body across it
at one end and puts her head down

and rolls up and down—over
the rough polyester and the thick
cotton, the worn dish towel
and the smooth kitchen cloth, and
yes, even over the ones given
to them at their wedding—
until her skin tingles and her
nose is caught with the scent
of fabric softener, and she knows
this room will never be the same
again. No, this house cannot be
the same after it has shown
the possibility of such pleasure.

## The heart of my house

is a hallway, wide as my husband's arms
where I paste pictures of the past
upon the pink walls and wonder
if this is still where we belong.
Are we the same couple who crept
under radar to cling to each other
for safety, bringing us safely
to a place where we could be children,
ourselves, before having one? My heart
beats outside myself now, in this hallway
between two bedrooms, between a toddler's
tantrums and the tom-tom rhythm of a teenager's drum.

So only soft, in the night, can the sound
of the skin of his hand in mine on our wedding night
still be heard in this hallway, my heart,
between the children who sleep while I paint
a new picture—the blue shadow of us, older,
one day, but still lit from within with hope—
next to the one of us, already fragile and fading,
when we were just beginning our long slide
down this small hallway starting to slope.

## A Hungry Wife

1.
The joy I feel
when I touch
your hip
in the dark
is the knowledge
that my body
is bread
and you can eat
this simple meal
and be satisfied.

2.
Taste the time
we have together.
It is not long.
Nothing is.

3.
I want more.
I want to fill
to be full
to be filled
to be.

4.
In my dream
I saw people starving.
They wanted bread
every day—
only bread.

5.
I want bread
and basil,
bread and chocolate,
bread and butter,
bread and wine.
Am I selfish?

6.
This hunger
of knowing
there must be more
keeps me moving
toward the unseen
source.

7.
Sometimes I feel
I've had enough
and we sleep
soundly.

8.
Faith is knowing
I will want more
in the morning.

9.
I am
your joy
and this is
my livelihood.
We need
to invent
words
for this.

10.
I am
a hungry
wife.

## The beginnings of rain

One day I stopped trying, frying, and buying
goods for the house. I stepped back from countertops,
let the crumbs wilt, and listened
from behind walls to the sounds of heaving.
My family, motherless, giving birth to itself,
My husband, screeching, like I used to do,
at all he had to do before the next errand.
And the children, coming to him,
as they used to do to me, with knees
bleeding, tummies hungry and bodies
to be put to bed. And I listened,
from behind walls, to the winds inside
my own skin, shut the windows of my fingers,
refused to lift a hand, heard the storm stirring,
clouds converging over my own dry land,
and listened to the beginnings of rain.

## Hurricane Season

Facing southeast, I wait for the hurricane,
feel the purple wind on my cheeks,
know that nothing will be the same.

I have ridden the air on an eastern rug,
woven with blood and memory,
and the colors still cling to my skin.

I am not afraid of the seasons,
not the mountains or rivers or night.
I am one desert pink flower in bloom.

And when my summer is over,
I will return to the earth with gratitude,
lay my petals upon her damp breast,

and know that nothing is ever the same.
I have lived, bloomed, given birth,
died, all in my own name, all in my name.

## To catch a falling leaf

It is very hard
to catch a falling leaf,
but if you sit still
long enough,
they will fall
and fill your lap.

## There is a room

in my mind that opens
onto leaves of oak
and hands, and here
my heart expands
with wonder, knowledge
that I have always been
and always will be
myself.

                     This
is the gift of healing,
the wholesomeness that moves
through the round world
in the room
that is my help,
my shelf,
my body,
my self.

## Wishes

the wind across your porch
the rose and its cycles
your husband's patience
your children's laughter
how flowers prosper
sunlight
a turtle in your yard
lizards on white wood
African dance
letters from friends
books you get lost in
how leaves come and go
the opposite of pain
wind from the North in summer
wind from the South in winter
wind from the West most days
wind from the East when we need rain
butterflies in daylight
moths at moon
dragonfly
hawk
philosophy
dreams
hunger
food

## This is my disease

This is my disease: wishing.
The dice in the hand, the breath,
the roll. These are the symptoms.
I cough up luck.
I burn with the fever
of what could be better.
I am sleepless
with the possibility
of dreams.
And you, my doctor,
sit at my bedside
and make plans.
You write up budgets
for me to follow.
You make me sign papers
and mail them to me
in triplicate.
Nothing works.
I refuse
to be cured.
I throw all my pennies in the fountain,
and then jump in.
You throw up your hands.

## Reunion

We walked
from deserts, islands, ghettos, suburbs, our fathers' homes
through the cold night, down into the pink room
where our sisters talked and waited, even until the end
for the arrival of all the others who were not yet there.

I looked
at the faces, the bodies, watched for lines of pain and signs
of torture from the road. Some were visible, some heard
in silences filled with smiles or an embrace, held
a little song, a little clinging, in thanksgiving for having arrived.

We gathered
for a picture, touched each other, laughed, stared, smiled
into mirrors, into men who loved us, reflected us in our love
who were as functional as cameras recording our love
for each other, someone to say, I was there, I saw it, too.

I whispered
into your ear my quick secrets, what I'd dreamed or awoke from
in the night, what I'd wanted to tell you all these years
we were apart, how many times I'd said your name and wondered
where you were and why you were so far from me.

We talked
confidently, all together, to women close who would listen, talked
in words strong with knowing we were listening, talked together,
told of deaths of fathers and lovers and sisters still missing,
talked in ways we cannot speak outside that room.

I cried
later for the shadows of the women still moving on the wall, as the bodies leave
and the spirits linger, split between the desert of our father's home
and the embrace of our sisters in the underground room. We are split between
ourselves out here just as surely as we were together in that room.

We wait
for each other as we put away the clothes and write the thank-you notes
and pick the child up from school and get into bed next to men. We wait
for the road that will take us back to that final pink room where we will talk
and embrace and love each other, finally, unafraid, never needing to return.

## Her Colors

Her colors wrap around the canvas like diapers.
The pin, cutting baby flesh, leads to bleeding.
The anger of accidental pain. The kind of red.

And the yellow, barely making it,
the way sunlight never really reaches through
the window near a hospital bed.

The lavender, on stems, stored away for seasons,
in a drawer, dry and brittle, fading.
Just a hint of scent remaining.

The orange, sad. Like a bitter woman, tired of waiting.
Not afraid to tell you. Not afraid to be mad.

And the black, moving. Like people
you thought you knew, but didn't.
The ones who moved into and out of you, without touching.
That kind of black.

And the pink. The lipstick of a thirteen-year-old.
In her room, alone. Looking in the mirror,
hoping her mother won't come in.
Tracing, tracing her lips, deeper,
deeper into brightness. Into leaving.

And the green. The green of mint, of wind, of sage,
of wanting. The green you make yourself for fear
it will not grow this season. The green out of season.
The green of making your own season.

White, fenced in. Circles, squares, lines, shapes.
Holding the smoke so it doesn't smother.
Keeping it checked. Boundaried. Safe.
Staying awake. A discipline. A limit.
Snow shoveled before it has time to drift.

All the colors together make brown,
but darker, deepened by years of waiting.
In mirrors, at diapers, over dinners.
And finally the break.

For cream. The leaking of dreams.
The sudden shift. Motion.
The churned middle of an eclair, bit down, oozing.
Taking seconds. Thirds.
That kind of rapture.
That kind of color.

## My daughter at 4 asks about war

Cupping her two blue eyes above water,
she asks, "Mommy, why is there a bird in our yard?"
and I know what she means. "It's a dove
on a sign for peace," I say. "We don't want war."

"Fighting?" she asks, and I nod, wait for more.
"Some people swim like this," she says, belly flat
on the white bottom, and then suddenly pulling
her knees underneath, "and some people swim like this."

"It's different," she concludes, and I think of the frog
green lights I saw on television a decade before,
imagine children in bathtubs stretched out beneath
mothers, or crouching, like this, just as the bombs hit

and they disappeared, like her brother did, inside me,
during that war, unplanned but still wanted, unlike
this one, so planned but unsure. What power we have
over death, I think, just because we are alive

and still living, and I want to give her something more,
more than a sign against war, more than a memory
of a brother, more than my visions of death, something
of peace she can keep, as she swims, with resolution,
free in her skin, in this water, already so rapidly
moving away, already so far from the shore.

## This Bird

1.
What is this bird, who scratches, camouflaged in the colors of papers
that have been scattered and burned? See how it hops, in reverse,
to search for its food? And then, another. And another again.
A trinity of birds outside my window, jumping on crippled feet
through the crinkly leaves—and a voice whispers in me,
I am that bird. And this. And this. All three.

2.
I am female. I am male. I am juvenile.
I am a family, the entered and the entering,
and the baby they hope to feed long enough to survive.

3.
There must be a story about this, a legend or myth—
something to tell me how a woman can also be a man,
how a human can also be a bird, how a body can also be a word,
so I look, and find only the generic (for "bird," I find Horus) attached to a name.
I look in book after book for "sparrow," and find only spider and snake.
There must be more to being a woman, I think, so I keep searching,
and at last, I turn to the Bible. On the left is the sparrow sacrificed in Leviticus,
and on the right, she is lowly and afraid.

4.
I close all the books and look again out the window.
A female cardinal taps on the glass with that beak, so peach, so yellow, and says,
Write your own book.
Hop backwards until you find food.
Build your nest on the ground.
Live for today, not tomorrow.
Tend to your eggs, no matter your mood.

**The fear**

The fear      is what holds you back

like gravity

to the earth of your past

fly

I say

you do not believe

you can

move into the fear

with wings

of words

and you will rise      into the skies

of your life

like a bird

discovering

her voice

for the first time.

## Uncoupling from my husband

Even as I realize
how interwoven my
body has become
with yours, over years
of knowing what
comes next, each move
we make while nude,
and all we have forgotten—
the fresh uncertainty of desire—
I move purposefully away from
this old knowledge, slide
like a small boat
into the great sea,
not knowing what wave
or weather will be
there to greet me, but happy
to taste the tears and salt
with my own tongue,
ready to find out again
the joy of discovery,
the promise of fear itself,
as I allow myself to be
undone, and vow no longer
to have to do it myself.

## Leaving

This is my last
time here with you.
We sit in the green
world and let go
into blue. I am
afraid. Fear is
a stomach ache.
I know why kids
wake up in the night.
I want you
to rub my back.
I want you
to sing to me.
I want the day
to start over.
I never want
to go to sleep.
I am fragile.
I could break.
Hold me like a baby.
Feed me. Tell me
we are not making
a big mistake.

## Red is the color of the year

Red is the color of the year
when, with great sadness,
you will leave your bags in doorways
of your life, and hail a trail,
and not look back at what you leave behind,

and laugh, and let the path come to take you.
You will go to the land *de flor y canto*.
Do not give up if at first
you do not find them.
Keep walking. Keep crying. Keep believing

in your voice. It will lead you
to the corner of a thousand red carnations.
Buy a dozen. Buy red chilis. Smell them both.
They are the smell of your new life.

## My skin became a touchable thing

I borrowed clothes,
and thought I was someone
        different.        I was accepting

compliments for who
I seemed to be
            becoming.

But I shivered,
in blue and black
layers of sweater.

I could not get warm
until I took it off.
                    And then my skin
became a touchable thing. Like the selkies
who find warmth
in the wet        water
                    of their true seal
        covering.

                    I dove, deep,
and found another body,            my own,
waiting for me,
            after all these years,

young
            and on fire
not with what was

            or would be
                possible,
but in the presence
of what was being        given
just then.

## The Willow

There was a willow tree in my childhood,
and my sister and I hid under its branches
while our father hit our mother
and we recited the Hail Mary and imagined
that we were children in the Garden
of Eden, and that God and Jesus and Mary,
our trinity, were waiting somewhere nearby.

The willow tree was bare last night,
as I contemplated the complexities
of husbands and lovers and daughters
and mothers, and the chances of how I can be
something other than what I had been.
The willow's branches pointed down, in the dark,
and I thought I'd always miss the mark.

But this morning the tiny green shoots point up,
and I realize we, too, are always coming
and going like this—away from our childhoods
or back to them, hiding from the new selves
we are becoming, or rushing to embrace them,
like magnets flipping through the seasons
around the roots of the willow at the center of the earth.

## Summer solstice

I sit, half naked, in the greening
yard, pulsing blood, taking shards
from my childhood, putting back
together what I can remember.

My fingers bleed, spurt onto the glass
as I glue the colors onto wood,
make a mosaic of what could
never be again, and bury it, dead.

There are some memories too damp
to ever dry, so we cut away
the sog until a fly with wings remains
and flutters over crimson stains.

And still the turning of the sun
is witness to what survives undone;
though hidden in the clouds, he glows
and beats a rhythm for what still grows.

## Blue is a tongue in the snake of nature

Blue is a tongue in the snake of nature
where the mouth of the day opens for first light,
and inside hang, hidden, coats of teeth to cover
the gloom of the fast and fading night.

I want to be the snake who opens
and with my bite of words to heal
what is lying broken on the roadside,
that, when chewed, becomes
what only splinters can reveal.

There is a cave in Mexico
where, it is said, the gods were born.
This is a story for the present,
for all who feel their lives are torn.

We must learn to enter mouths
of snakes and caves and canyons
so to begin anew. With each ending
is an opening. With each black night,
the promise of the blue.

## Lilith

If I were a color, I would be
the waxy edge of a red apple,
I would be its round slope down,
I would roll. Quietly.
Like a snake. Humming
her desert song in the forest,
coming upon a lake
in the middle of trees
and sinking in for shelter.
I let go of my airy habitat
for wetness, remember the sand
and I dive deeper into blue,
want to be free in the new,
want to pop like a water lily
from the center of the pool.

## Eat Life

Like caramel,
scoop it out
with your fingers.
Let it drip
down your tongue.
The sweet,
the chew,
the warm and melt,
eat it all.
When you are old,
gum it.
Smile
while you nod
at offerings
of seconds.
Ignore the stares
from those who starve
around you.
You must eat.
Picture all you want
that they cannot even
imagine.
Let the juice spill.
Let your mouth be covered,
shiny,
with what you've carried
to your lips.
Let life fill you
with tastes
each day.
Let your throat
be wet.
Let your life
be fed.

## Stretch

1.
The frame of my bed
is a boat that carries me
over the sea of dreams.
It does not matter
who is beside me
while I sleep
for I carry the sacred bodies
of the whole world
inside me
while I dream.

2.
Sacred?
Did I say sacred?
I meant scared.

I meant my dream
is a nightmare.

I meant
they are
the same.

3.
I thought once
when you looked into my eyes
we were the same.

4.
But what comes between us
(air, distance, the night, your lies,
my endless hesitation)
is the same as what brought us together
that time.

5.
It is
the separation
that makes coming
together
possible.

6.
I once saw a hawk in Mexico
it flew
in circles
above me
and I was
with it,
as if a single thread
stretched
through the air
between us.
It was
the stretch
that made this
possible.

7.
But before the stretch
comes the hard work
of wishing.
The long work
of "as if"
that must be laid out
like tile
to make the walk
across
possible.

8.
And the final stretch
will be an ending
that takes us
beyond
where we
have been.
It is beyond breath,
this stretch,
and so we must
return to the beginning.

9.
One morning
I woke
to find
a year

had gone by
and I
was a different
person.

10.
And so it goes, again.
The stars
above
still spin
in their own
separate
season.

And I
am not yet one
but must
begin
somehow
to let
my own
star
shine
from the inside
with
(or
without)
you
now.

## Exile

I know how long a flood can last;
I've felt it rising up in me long past
the forty days of fleeing, forty nights
of dreaming drier days in exile.

It has been one hundred and fifty
days since I last saw my husband
on the land we called our home;
this is why tears have salt—a memory

can be as wide as the ocean.
Even Noah, after the ark perched
upon the mountain top, still waited,
and sent out his birds for signs.

The first bird was the raven—that black,
stubborn thing. I felt it fly from me,
too, as I searched in the night for new
arms to hold me as I wept.

It kept flying, found no home,
and so Noah had to give up, and turn
to another bird. The dove of peace
rose up from my fingertips as I touched

the numbers on the phone and heard
my husband's voice, soft and open,
yet far away. His mouth was holding
the olive branch, and yet my ark

had landed and I was too tired
to make the journey back again,
so soon. This is where forty days
come in. Days of waiting where you've

landed, days of knowing you have
no plan. Days of birds, and faith, and
that awful knowledge that what will
happen next is out of your hands.

## Persephone

Surely, all of this
cannot be for me.

The wasp who flies
like a cripple,
making lines in the air.

The robin on the
green grass, always
looking down.

The cicadas in the tree
above, getting louder,
telling me to pay attention.

The hissing cry of the hawk
in the woods, where
I can't see her.

The grasshopper near the
butterfly bush, grown
so large he just sits there.

And butterflies,
tipping into their drinks,
loveliest drunks in nature.

And further, seven heads
of green buds of roses,
with nothing to do but wait.

And more flowers I cannot name,
orange, yellow, red, and purple.

Did my mother miss me
this much, that she did all this in celebration?

## Demeter

Yes, child, I did miss
the way your little hand
touched my neck
and I felt my breath
go into you
and we were one.
How, naked from the bath,
I would lift you up
above my head
so you could feel
how far you would grow
and we would laugh
at how long
you had to go.
How the day
you saw the snake
and thought it was a twig
you were not afraid
but blinked
when you saw its tongue
flickering.
No, child, there is no way
for you to know
how much my anger rose
at your departure,
how the womb of the world
closed.

How I cut the roses
to their core
to have no reminder.
How, like the wheat,
I lay, yellow,
waiting
for knives
to cut me.
And how, when no knife came,
I rose like a bee
from the ground
and began to hover.
The breeze
in a seastorm
was not as loud
as my whine.
And just when the bronze
jars, filled with my tears,
thick as honey,
were to overflow,
the old woman came
to tell me I must spill them.
And where they flowed
would grow poppies.
Red were my poppies,
and small,
when your fruit burst
back upon the earth.
You had grown
so tall,

you could look into
my eyes
and I
into yours
and together
our tears
shone equally.
Who is to say
which is worse:
to be abandoned
by a daughter
or abducted
by a man.
May you never know both.
Oh, daughter
become mother,
I watch you
in the moon,
grow and give birth
and flow
away again.
Yes, daughter,
I missed you
this much,
that I would give
the grain and the wind,
the flowers and the rain
to your son,
born of my sorrow
to eat.

## Women

We are women in stone,
our bodies hard
as history untold.

And a violin plays in the background,
held by lemon blossom hands,
the music of hair and wind and skin.

We write with our legs.
We sing with our hands.
We dance with our faces above the clouds.

We come in colors,
sherbet and earth,
sepia and green.

Our breasts are eyes for what we have never seen.
We are young, new like daylight, and old, worn like guns.
We are strong and still, the gloss of our backs in six suns.

We laugh.
We lead armies. We cry.
We bear sons. We rejoice.

We raise daughters,
those that are born
and those we become.

## What the meadows made me remember

I landed upon green fields, and the meadows
made me remember that movement is not only
about leaving, and beginning again, but that I
can be like the flowers that stay in one place
from the brown sweep of winter into the shy
green of spring before bursting into color
and starting all over again. When the voice
of the meadow speaks, you should listen.
So I did. I lay my weary body down
in the same place I'd earlier wanted
to escape, and I waited for life to come in.

## The Prodigal Wife

I went to the garden to look for what I had lost.
The beauty berry, the red peppers, the moss—
all greeted me as I walked
through the green October—blooming and dying—
garden.

    And there were children.
The voices of them, learning to speak,
returned me to the memory of my own breast milk
which I'd spilled, happily, here
in this garden.

    That was a long time ago.
And here, in the autumn, I return, again and again,
to the smell of the rose,
craving something sweet in the midst
of all this seeding.

    I sit, alone,
near the canna in bloom, and prepare to lie down
with my husband, his face like the rosemary
that scratches my fingers, his lips
like the hardy marigold that tickles my skin
as I kiss the green and the smell remains
on my hands long after I return from the garden,
long after the garden
        teaches me how to begin again.

### How to return to your husband

Find a spot that is sunny.
Let the breeze touch your face.
Stop running. Let your heart
stay in one place. Look
at what you have together
already done. It is not over.
You are both new now,
and you have come a long way.
But continue. Have faith
in what has already begun.

## Say the words

There are a thousand prayers
that arise each moment
as we wonder what path
to take, as we stand
and watch others leaving,
as we hold our own hands
under the heat of the sun
and wait for it all to be done.
It has all been solved,
I hear a voice say, as light
comes in the window
and I think of how far
we have come: you, from
the dark hole in your heart,
me, from my own blind need.
We have both been freed.
What good is prayer, you ask,
if it's all been given?
Not given; solved, I reply.
The prayers are necessary
for the solutions to find
their way in. This part
is something you can do:
Say the words
so God will know
how to reach you.

## I dream of the day when we will

set fire to the jewelry stores and watch them burn,
and when the ashes cool, dig through them to find
older stones—that we will not carve
into shapes for our fingers, but will
keep whole and circle them around us,
around our whole bodies and watch
the sun and moon and know that
we should never carry jewels again,
that we are the jewelry of the world,
as we sit on the hand and watch
to see what time will carry us into,
as we spin, like a ring on a finger,
round and round, awaiting this,
the final end of that old story—
for this, not hope, we lie out here;
for this we were born,
for this, not God, is dying.

## Seasons

A year ago, I ate the seed
and waited for the flowers
to sprout from my fingers.
They came out as weeds.
Bore thorns. My skin wept
with white tears, at what
I had lost, what still needed
to come out and be buried.
But the first flowers,
their fruits, are not the last
harvest. It takes seasons
to know the strength of the
root. Seasons. Do you
understand what this means?
Never despair at what grows
from the depths of your spirit.
You do not know what mineral
you might bear, what tree
might become sturdy beams.
Keep growing. Soon cotton
and wheat will burst from your seams.

## The Fragile Iris

1.
Spring.
The gentle pink blueberry bush is blossoming.
Morning leaves shimmer in gold light.
Hope for things that are real.
Live in service of an ideal.
Do what is right.

2.
Birds are busy. Scratch. Flit. Tweet.
You watch. Cut an apple. Eat.
How can you write about pain without feeling it?
You can't. Admit this. Declare defeat.

3.
Below you, a shadow. Look up, a hawk.
Veers away.
A turn in the road.
From despair to meaning.
One bow. One harp.
Harmony from darkness is sharp.

4.
Balsam, basil, yellow evening primrose.
Moonflower seeds from last year's harvest face death.
A bluebird with a yellow aura flies away to the forest.
And then comes back.
Its underbelly is red.
Three crows fly overhead.

5.
The Moonlight Sonata is grasses up close,
butterfly bombers, small children
on swings, birds without wings,
thunderstorm clouds, the air rolling in.
All that we miss by not paying attention.

6.
I was awake.
I am awake again.
Floods of stillness, giving way to the dawn.
The first fragile purple iris, large and heavy, tips from the weight of itself.
Hold to the thread.
Lift your head.

7.
Clematis pink butterflies clap hello on the porch.
Mommy, mommy, mommy.
Look at me.
The early lily is spent.
But the iris has new buds developing, lower down.

8.
Our words have histories,
magic we evoke
when we say them.
They arrive
unblemished.

They shine.
They are surprised, though,
when sometimes
we do not remember them.

9.
Send the letters.
Say what we want love to banish.
Say what we want love to bring.
The first dew of an oak tree before dawn, caught in a jar.
The tree, old and wise. The dew, wet and small.
Both are unafraid to sing.

10.
Time to separate: the first iris is brown and dry and withered.
The second iris has bloomed, deeper lavender, supple.
And the third
is in bud,
dark purple
curled in
on itself,
waiting.

11.
Ancestors chirp, reassure.
The past
is filled with horrors
I cannot control.

The future
is filled with uncertainty
I cannot know.
The present
is a cool
beautiful wet warm
soft firm space
I can fill.
Time
now
to live it.

## A Garden

I have eaten the poverty
of weeds, taking what was
left over. Dandelion,
kudzu, moss. I have chewed
on them for years. My mouth
and hands are green from loss.

I want a garden.
Borders and beds,
bright corners and a bench
in the shade. I want water
daily. I deserve this.

I know there is a gardener
who can give it. A place
where I can sit down
and rest. I am ready
to find it. Such gifts
are not merely a matter
of money. They start

in nature's heart—
with labor so sweet it sings
a harmony of honey,
work so hard it continues
long after dark.

## A Mother Greets the Dawn

Lavender against the white foundation,
crepe myrtle beside the yellow
clapboard house; these are
the colors of my garden, what
surround me when I go out
from the dishes and the papers
and the clothes lying strewn
about, and the bodies of my daughter
and my husband, still asleep,
closed-mouthed. The trumpet vine
and vinca wait for summer sun
to poke her head above the tops
of green, but I hide. I hide
like the blackberries, plump
and dark and juicy, soon to be
eaten, but for now, unseen.
This is where I give birth
to someone other
than who I have been.

## Still I Worry

Four doves dip and sway
and a cardinal finds its nest.
I wonder where I'm going
and how long I need to rest.

The birdfeeder hangs empty
and the sweet gum tree
is gone. These were
under my control—
not the bluebird's song.

God says, Seek
and you will find me.
Still I worry
that my choices
might be wrong.

Sun rises.
Crow caws.
How simple.
It was in me
all along.

## Butterfly Song

I am the mistress of folding.
See my wings in the rhythm

of wind: opening, closing,
each moment, now, no end.

You can do this, too,
despite your heavy limbs.

Open yourself to miracles.
Open yourself to love.

The eyes of a stranger.
The rain from above.

Close yourself to danger.
Close yourself to hate.

Follow your own instincts.
Know when to lock your gate.

I am the mistress of folding.
You can be, too. Rise above

what is blind to your beauty.
Dip into your deepest need.

Soar beyond duty.
Dip into the core of you.

## The Poemgranate

It is fall, the time after the beginning.
Not spring, not one thing in its infancy.
No fantasy of pregnancy or baby again.

I am in a hotel room, far from home.
Next door a baby cries. The mama
Coos her sweet southern comfort.

I did this with you, when you were young.
I ran like Persephone, but with a baby,
Smoky Mountains, New Mexico plains,

Boston, and beaches—we've seen the insides
Of hotel rooms turned tombs as I tried
To get what all mothers want, peace

And quiet. I would put you on the floor,
My lily, my orchid, my crocus, let you
Play with plastic cups, suck from multiple

Bottles, anything for one moment
When I could look away without fear
Of falling or choking or hurt.

It is fall, the time after the beginning.
Not spring, not one thing in its infancy.
No fantasy of pregnancy or baby again.

You are no baby anymore, at eight
You have fallen from grace
Many times—not from your mother

But from yourself, which is worse.
I mourn like Demeter, even though
You are still here. You inherited

More than my eyes: my vision,
My moods, my hungers, my cycles
And sins. They live in your skin.

You told me last week you had waited
For thousands of years in the sky
For a mother who would take you in.

Me, I said, smiling, I was the best one.
And then you stuck in the pin: No,
You were the only one to be so dumb.

It is fall, the time after the beginning.
Not spring, not one thing in its infancy.
No fantasy of pregnancy or baby again.

I have no flowers to welcome you back,
No seeds to plant, no chants to make
You whole again. I am human.

Not a goddess with magic or power
To create seasons that mirror
My immense sorrow, your great need.

All I can do is to feed my desire
For solitude, find a way back
To myself through these words

That I harvest like fruits, plucked
From my head, cut open in bed,
And eaten, forbidden or not,

Seeds and core, peel and stem, entire.
It is with this poemgranate that I might
Make myself, mother, whole again.

## No Answer

Sunlight on the pine in the forest,
mockingbird sings her crazy song.
Cardinals rustle in oaks
to the south. It is just after dawn.
I am facing west, the land
of water, emotion and tears.
But I feel nothing. No sadness,
frustration or fears. Is this
a good thing, I ask,
looking up to the sky.
Purple martins dip and sway,
halfway up to clouds.
No answer. No cry.
Just birds who continue to sing.
And one dove, by herself
on the power line. Quiet.
No worries. Not one single thing.
Maybe this is my answer
when I look for a sign:
search inside myself,
and find peace. Watch
the birds that surround me,
and know, the way nature knows,
that this life is perfectly fine.

## Pay Attention

Chickadee in the birdfeeder watches me nervously as he gathers seeds, then takes them up into the tree, hidden by leaves, and thanks me with clicks and chirps. A woodpecker flies north, high, cracking his throat. And a cardinal boy zooms past, low to the grass, to the south. A large bird lands in the cherry tree and makes a throaty warble—something I've not heard before. I look up from my writing. It's a blue jay, the Cherokee symbol of blind ambition, looking down on the feeder, and asking for more. The crazy mockingbird sings louder than anyone, high in the pine. He even tries to sound like a hawk, scaring the birds with a loud whine. It works. For a while, no one comes. They hide in their nests, and only scurries of squirrels can be heard. Then a hawk, a real one, spreads his red wings and silently lands in the sweet gum. Complete quiet. A slight breeze. The sky clouds over. Rain later. But for now, I sit here, learning my lesson: Pay attention to truth, from wherever it comes. You never know what crazy bird it might emerge from.

## Insomnia

Eyes watery from fatigue and the smoke of sage and tobacco, I bend over the altar I made with my own fingers long ago. I made it, then, for now, when I would need it, in the night, when even after an Ambien and a picture of Jesus beside me, I cannot sleep. The streetlight goes out and the crickets stop singing. Sometimes it is only when you miss something that you notice it was there. Their song is related to light, I think with one side of my brain, but the opposite hand keeps writing, like the crickets' song that goes on after a minute of dark. They have found a new rhythm, and then the light comes on again, and they sing louder than ever, their faith restored in the world and its patterns. How I want to be like the creatures who sing together and are not afraid of the noise that they make. How is it that they know what to do, in silence, and how long to wait to begin the next chorus? So I listen, and this time I notice there is a leader who makes the first note, tells the others it's okay to begin. I need this leader inside me, to tell me to stop when there is danger and I start to spin. So I call on Jesus and Buddha, St. Francis, Teresa, Kali, Great Spirit, Yahweh, Tara, The Virgin of Guadalupe, Lakshmi, Durga, Mary, my mother, her mother, all the ancestors and the earth, asking them to teach me to sleep, let rest kick in, not give in to the manic pulsing of my heart. Let their voices be my leader cricket, telling me when to stop and start. I've seen miracles. And I know that the way they work is to let them, surrender to a friend or go where anything can happen, and it does, and you are not in control, someone else is, something much greater. It comes. And you rest into realizing how big this life is, there is a chorus, there is light, there is dark, and you, like the cricket, play only a part.

## Claiming My Territory

Fox came from the east,
approached the yard,
then stared at me.

I stood up in the dark.
She growled.
I backed down.

Still growling,
she circled the house.
This time

I decided
to protect myself,
claim my territory,

show my dominion,
a small piece of land
and a house,

nothing more.
I am not greedy,
but I protect what is mine

so I pulled the dragon
from inside the closet—
what the therapist

had given my daughter
to battle her fears—
and went back to the porch,

pulled the cord
and let it roar.
No sign of the fox,

dragon's eyes glowing red,
a voice deep and loud,
and behind me,

an open door.
I went back inside,
lit a candle,

settled against a wall
with pillows on the floor.
Pinch of tobacco

on the windowsill,
a breeze blows in
from the garden

I'd planted
days before:
purple petunia

and double begonia.
Birds start to wake.
It's 4:24.

A new day beginning,
the summer sun glowing.
Who could ask for more?

Calm now,
I breathe out,
put the candle

back on its shelf,
crawl into bed
with the dragon,

finally learning
to take care
of myself.

## And this is what I have to learn

And this is what I have to learn, still: to be open
to what is being given. To keep quiet. Let love
come back to me. I want to chase it down. Use
tools. A hammer. Facilitate the capture. I want
to win. It makes me nervous to do nothing.
I'd rather peck on the ground, my beak bleeding,
looking for seeds. When will I learn that this world
is a farmyard, and coming in a bucket
to be scattered before me is everything I need?

## 16 names for love

A clean floor.
Air.
A lizard by the door.
What is fair.
A long look.
Food.
That book.
A new mood.
Hunger.
The opposite of doubt.
Stepping from danger.
Tears coming out.
Your eyes.
Saying my name.
Blue skies.
More of the same.

## There is a worship

It is easy to love
the flowers that spring
unwanted through the concrete.
Their strength. Their daring.
What's not to respect?

But there is a worship
I am trying to achieve:
to love the sidewalk.

To love what was useful
but crumbles, is destroyed
by the force of beauty,
her never ceasing need.

## Returning to the true

I have been in a cave,
known how rock walls can secure,
how a dark winged creature can be a friend.
I came out into the light,
wanted to see how night might end.

I have been in a tree,
seen beauty at great distance,
learned the freedom of dawn's song.
But I came down from those branches,
wanted to know how it feels to belong.

I have been in a house,
felt the comfort of a bed,
known the company that dishes keep.
I moved out eventually,
wanted to feel the ground beneath my feet.

I am returning to the true, I
know it is not found on any map.
I will travel there alone, holding
lightly onto those who are with me.
I will no longer mistake my place
as the only purpose of this journey.

## I Wait for Sunrise in the Dark

Before me in the south stand three trees,
each one a bit taller than the other,
working right to left,
the opposite of writing
in this language of the west,
or the correct way in the east—
toward the sun in the morning,
as I wait for sunrise in the dark.
The sky is brighter than midnight,
but still I could see nothing
if it weren't for lamplight
and my candle, talismans
against the beating of my heart.
I breathe, like the trees,
through my fingers, on these
leaves of paper, reaching
for the sky—that silent height
within me, where soft air surrounds
my body, like a gentle breeze
on a summer morning after a long rain
that has come and gone, and now only good
things—peace and dawn—float by.

## Everything is art

Everything is art,
my life has taught me.
Even goblins, even trees.
Even bleeding tongues
and dirty knees.

Everything sings its song
until we learn it, cry it
out in castle lullabies,
like my thumbs pressed
hard upon my eyes,

and the patterns
that it makes.
It is a painting.
There are colors,
fear, and time,

captivity and freedom.
It is the combination
of pain and singing
that make a decoration.
Everything is art.

## Sorting Stones

There are stones lying in the yard.
It is your job to gather them, sort the colors
of your life. Blue, the days that passed
without awareness, the sense of floating
in the air. These were the days you missed,
and long for, on red days, the ones when anger
rattles rusty pins. Your blood spins
against itself, crying out for green,
the breath, the beat of growth, each time
you look behind and see where
you have been. Yellow, the need
for reassurance, the letter in the mailbox
that never comes, the expectation, breath.
Black, the night when, dreamless,
you wish for some passing, a star,
a car, and nothing. Orange, jump up
and sing, what you never knew
you wanted arrives and drives
you further than you ever thought
you'd go. Purple, the people
who will come to your funeral,
the words they will say, you hear
them now, in the silence, in the stones
surrounded in white, all the hard
and beautiful moments of your life.

## Walking With My Daughter

Past where the blackberries used to sing,
now gone to feed the mockingbird, nuthatch
and wren—or gone to seed—already
the summer takes wing. We walk
the outer edge of the land.

We do not hold hands.
We bend to inspect the baby
sunflower hiding under the swing.
What a cardinal dropped on her way
to the nest and might grow now,
if given a chance, if left to rest.

It has taken me years, as a mother, to learn
what nature in her heart already knows.
To nurture another, walk together,
but slightly apart, not too close.
This is how living things grow.

## Hummingbird Is a Symbol of Joy

She chirps briefly at the rose of Sharon before I turn my head
and she whizzes by. I heard she is a symbol of joy. I saw her
years ago after we planted a scarlet bush for the daughter,
now eighteen. Then she was nine, and we were just married.
How much we have seen. After nine years the tree bends with
the weight of its blossoms, as high as our house, and the daughter,
almost as tall as her father, leaves for a faraway college in the fall.
She is no longer quiet around strangers, nor scrawny as a mouse.
The hummingbird is a baby, her chirp is short, her body still small
and afraid. She will learn over years like the daughter and I did, together,
to hover close to each other in kindness, and be strong, muscle growing
on bones that nature has laid, like a plan or a promise faithfully made.

## What I want to tell you about the rain
*(for my niece)*

There will be seasons of longing
as the earth, your mouth, your mind
cry out for water. Faith, in this time,
will shimmer as it beckons and disappears.

Suddenly it will come. Your tongue,
out the car window, will greet it.
You will gulp it, be greedy.
You forget all your fears.

And then you grow weary,
miss the bees and the birds
and the wide wave of sunlight.
All is puddles and tears.

This is the thing about rain
that I want to tell you:
It will come. It will go.
The sooner you learn this,
the better. I know.

## How the Rose Works

I get up—second night of sleeping soundly,
with only one brief awakening—past dawn.
The rose bush, already in the summer sun,
just glows. Some blossoms drying brown
on top, others down below, pinkly hot.
Birds flutter, twit, and sit. But I pay no mind.
My eyes watch the roses as I sip my tea and
feel fine. The rose does her work in silence,
like a writer or a yogi, focused and aware,
moves so slowly you can't see it unless patient
enough to sit for hours with a calm mind,
and simply stare. This is how I want to live
my life, still and balanced, yet always growing,
open to the cycles of bud and blooming,
full of beauty, roots deep, thorns for protection,
stalks strong with liquid flowing up to feed
the bees, emitting sweet perfume into the air.

## This Is Mothering

I want to enter your dreams at night like an ancient legend.
I want to be the heroine who rescues you from every demon.

I want to be the spring that returns your blood to warming
on the days you feel too cold and old to lift your head.

I want to be the sudden memory of an answer on a test.
I want to be your stomach full of milk and never hungry,

never worrying when it will next be fed. I want to be your bed
and follow you as you walk down city streets, an offering

of rest throughout your cellphone day. This is mothering:
this wishing for the impossible, a plenitude of never wanting.

We might as well wish to conquer death. We did, once,
before your first breath: turned nothing into something,

made a whole person out of skin and love. You were in us then,
and we were your everything, your cards and dice and luck.

## The Lessons to Be Learned From Birds

She comes to my feeder, so close I can reach her,
and I bow my head to show her she is my teacher.
My eyes roll up to watch her, slightly pink with
brown feathers, not as bright as her mate but still
beautiful, and better camouflaged than her brother.
My eyes face forward, have the human limitation
of looking ahead, or up or down. But she, with gold
eyes on the sides of her head, can see sideways,
knows who is coming, who waits to be next—
not behind her or lesser, as humans often assume
of those who follow us. She is simply one of
many, and she has the courage to tell us this.

## Surrender

The rose of Sharon, lightly lit
by the porch lamp outside
my window, surrenders
to its blossoms, hanging
with the weight of rain
in the dark before dawn.
I, inside, sit facing that
symbol, legs outstretched,
body resting, refusing
to give in to the gravity
of time or pain. They fade,
as air through the screen,
the first cool breath
of late summer, comes
into my mouth, and I
take it in, and then out
again, giving back what
I have been given, out
into the world, passing
on what I have learned
of resistance and relaxing,
and how they differ from
gently bending in full
bloom and returning
to the earth and the roots
from which we came.

## Her Body, Once Blossomed

I clean the wispy hairs on my daughter's brush
and imagine them lonely for her as I am
in the middle of the day, abandoned
in this quiet house, like brown shoes that
were worn and grown out. I hold one hair
up to the light and notice the end, breathing in
and seeing how even the smallest thing splits.

Just this morning I was thinking of the Virgin Mary
and that snake she steps upon,
and I found a lonely snake skin on
the dry hydrangea bush in my garden.
It had black and white stripes, and I
wonder at the danger and think of my daughter,
what I can leave for her, what she
might need from me once I am gone.

If I were a bottle washed up on the shore
of her body, once blossomed, I would give
her this message: the only danger in life
is the magenta inside that you try to hide.
Don't play any game, either of black or of white.
This leads to checkmate. Be you. Be all your hues.
This is not a sin. You cannot lose. You cannot lose.

## I Loved This Landscape Into Being

It was the house of my husband
once, but women gathered together
to make a plan. We would reclaim
the land through our loving.
Paula provided pink roses, said
they were hard like a marriage,
took work. Angela planted
crepe myrtle in front of the
bedroom, said to learn to keep
some things in the dark.
My mother-in-law cut back
briars around the foundation,
said get rid of what has hurt you,
this is a place to be safe.
We put in the rose of Sharon
for Laura, who was seven.
Now she is grown and the bush
is a tree as big as the house.
My husband laid sod and cut
trees—you know how men are—
they need space for their balls.
But then he gave me a rocking
bench big enough for the whole
family to sit on and see leaves fall.
We put in another rose of Sharon,
this time lavender, when my daughter
was born. Later my mother gave me
Saint Francis holding a bird,

and the birds like to sit on his head,
round and shorn. They have planted
their gardens, too, the birds:
yellow evening primrose,
sunflower, chokecherry tree,
morning glories and millet and beans.
I loved this landscape
into being, and when I die,
I will return here in dreams.
Yes, I received help, and yes,
I could not have done it alone.
But never underestimate
the power of a woman who decides
to claim the earth as her own.

## Lima Beans

Both my girls like lima beans.
At first I thought it was a fluke.

The first one didn't come from
my belly; I couldn't claim her

taste. But the second did:
I named her when she was

a lima bean in me. Last night
for supper I made lima beans

and kale. They ate it up
like chocolate. I hated it.

I spooned one bowl in me
slowly, like those skinny ladies.

My girls asked for seconds
and I scooped them more.

I did not know mothering
would be like this: giving

them what they want, letting
go of what we wished.

## Love You Longer

I have learned to love you longer
each year you have grown older.

I planted more seeds this year
than ever before. They linger

in their dark beds, overtaking
the kitchen table and making

me move somewhere else
to chop. I remember when

I first felt the shock of pause
after planting: you were in me,

and nine months was eternity.
Now twelve years are gone

and I rest in certainty
that the next twenty

will fly even faster.
Last year was my first

real harvest in the garden:
tomatoes, peppers, cabbage,

collards, broccoli. This year
I've added basil, squash,

sage, and beets. You hand me
a packet of sunflower seeds,

say, *The birds love these.*
I am surprised when I see

how big they are in my hand.
I imagine this summer you

will stand next to them,
now taller than I am.

Another lesson in loving you
longer, as long as I can.

## Woman Births Century at Midlife

Alphabet hangs in the sky, on the wall, in my room
in the dark before dawn, giving me words in languages
that rise and fall like civilizations or notes from a song:
Styx is the river of memory, *Res* are the things I forgot,
Age is what is waiting for me, Faith is becoming what
I am not. *Os* are my bones, already brittle, *Dia* is the day
still ahead. *Mort* is the death I belittle. *Nue* is my naked
belly, daily needing to be fed. No longer baby, and not
yet old woman, I stand poised on the brink of midlife.
I am learning from nature how to be human, to survive
and give birth, and at the same time, be the midwife.

**Cassie Premo Steele** is a Pushcart Prize nominated poet, monthly columnist at *Literary Mama*, and the author of many books and hundreds of poems, essays, and short stories on mothering, creativity, and living in harmony with the natural world. From her Co-Creating Studio along a little creek in South Carolina, she coaches people in person and long distance to use writing to foster balance, healing, and creative empowerment. Learn more about her writing and coaching and sign up to receive her Co-Creating newsletter at www.cassiepremosteele.com.

## Publication Credits

Grateful acknowledgment goes to the publications where these poems first appeared:

"To Survive and Give Birth, and Be the Midwife." Appeared in an earlier version as "In spring, the daughter blooms," *Literary Mama*, Birthing the Mother Writer column, March 10, 2012. http://www.literarymama.com/columns/birthingthemotherwriter/archives/2012/in_spring_the_daughter_blossoms.html.

"In the Image of Me." *The Mom Egg*, 10 (2012). http://www.themomegg.com.

"The truth is I am afraid." *Stone Highway Review*, 1:2 (edited by Amanda Hash and Mary Stone Dockery): 93. http://www.stonehighway.com/uploads/8/0/0/8/8008182/shr_issue_2.pdf.

"The Lessons to be Learned from Birds." *Kudzu Review*, 1 (Winter Solstice 2011): 57. http://kudzureview.com/1.1.pdf.

"The Willow." *EarthSpeak Magazine*, 9 (Autumn 2011): http://www.earthspeakmagazine.com/cassiepremosteele9.htm.

"Lima Beans." *vox poetica*, June 2, 2011. http://poemblog.voxpoetica.com/2011/06/02/lima-beans.aspx.

"A Hungry Wife." Contributor's Series 5: Dramatis Personae, *vox poetica*, May 30, 2010. http://poemblog.voxpoetica.com/2010/05/30/contributor-series-5-dramatis-personae-a-hungry-wife.aspx.

"Days of the Dead." Contributors' Series 2: Candy and Spirits, *vox poetica*, November 4, 2009. http://poemblog.voxpoetica.com/2009/11/04/contributor-series-2-candy-and-spirits-days-of-the-dead.aspx?ref=rss. Reprinted in *From 9/11 to a New Year*, edited by Annmarie Lockhart (unbound CONTENT, 2010): 39. Also appeared in *Blessed Bee*, (Fall 2003): 5.

"The Poemgranate." *vox poetica*, November 23, 2009. http://poemblog.voxpoetica.com/2009/11/23/the-poemgranate.aspx.

"How the Rose Works." *Serenity Prayers*, edited by June Cotner (Kansas City: Andrews McMeel Publishing, 2009): 48-49.

"The Gardener." *The Petigru Review* (Fall 2008): 31; 86.

"What I Want to Tell You about the Rain," *The Petigru Review* (Fall 2008): 31; 142.

"Here Is the Mother Awakening." *Miracles of Motherhood: Poems and Prayers for a New Mother*, edited by June Cotner (New York: Center Street, 2007): 133.

"The First Sea." *Sand, Sea and Sail: A Poetry and Prose Anthology*, edited by Tom Davis (Fayetteville, NC: Old Mountain Press, 2007): 36. Also appeared in *Journal of the Association for Research on Mothering*, 3:2 (Autumn 2001): 88.

"The moment of labor." *MotherVerse: A Magazine of Contemporary Motherhood*, 5 (January 2007): 41.

"There is a room." *MotherVerse: A Magazine of Contemporary Motherhood*, 5 (January 2007): 41.

"How to return to your husband." *Forever in Love*, edited by June Cotner (Kansas City: Andrews McMeel, 2006): 87.

"A Mother Greets the Dawn." *In the Yard: A Poetry Anthology*, (Fayetteville, NC: Old Mountain Press, 2006): 77.

"There is a worship." *Pocket Prayers*, edited by June Cotner (Chronicle Books, 2006).

"The Prodigal Wife." *Literary Mama*, March 2006. http://www.literarymama.com/poetry/archives/2006/02/the-prodigal-wife.html.

"My skin became a touchable thing." *Literary Mama*, November 2004. http://www.literarymama.com/poetry/archives/2004/10/my-skin-became-a-touchable-thing.html.

"The Beginnings of Rain." *Fire in the Womb: Mothers and Creativity*, edited by Elizabeth Anderson and Kate Smith-Hanssen (Xlibris, 2003): 6. Also appeared in *Literary Mama*, January 2004. http://www.literarymama.com/poetry/archives/2003/12/the-beginnings-of-rain.html.

"Lilith." *Fire in the Womb: Mothers and Creativity*, edited by Elizabeth Anderson and Kate Smith-Hanssen (Xlibris, 2003): 45.

"Birthday Poem." *Fire in the Womb: Mothers and Creativity*, edited by Elizabeth Anderson and Kate Smith-Hanssen (Xlibris, 2003): 56. Also appeared in *AveNews* (February/March 2002): 13.

"Memory." *Fire in the Womb: Mothers and Creativity*. Edited by Elizabeth Anderson and Kate Smith-Hanssen. (Xlibris, 2003): 64. Also appeared in *AveNews* (April/May 2001): 6.

"In the Image of Me." *Fire in the Womb: Mothers and Creativity*, edited by Elizabeth Anderson and Kate Smith-Hanssen (Xlibris, 2003): 24.
"Walking on the Backs of Whales." *AveNews* (March/April 2000): 14. Also appeared in *Journal of the Association for Research on Mothering*, 3:2 (Autumn 2001): 54. Also appeared in *CALYX, A Journal of Art and Literature by Women*, Vol. 21, no. 2 (Summer 2003): 95.

"What I cannot tell you." *Journal of the Association for Research on Mothering*, 3:1 (Spring 2001): 19.

"The First Moment." *Proposing on the Brooklyn Bridge, Poems about Marriage*, edited by Ginny Lowe Connors (West Hartford, CT: Poetworks, A Division of Grayson Books, 2003): 76. Also appeared in *To Love One Another: Poems Celebrating Marriage*, edited by Ginny Lowe Connors. (West Hartford, CT: Poetworks, A Division of Grayson Books, 2002): 50.

"Spring, again." *Journal of the Association for Research on Mothering*, 3:1 (Spring 2001): 215.

"Red is the color of the year." *Knowing Stones: Poems of Exotic Places*, edited by Maureen Tolman Flannery (John Gordon Burke Publisher, 2000): 15.

"To catch a falling leaf." *Blessed Bee* 2 (Autumn 1999): 19.

"Wishes." *Blessed Bee,* 1 (Summer 1999): 24.

"The fires." *The Museletter: News and Resources from the National Association for Poetry Therapy.* 19:2 (July 1999): 18.

"Persephone." *The New Review,* 5 (1999): 40-41. Also appeared in *AveNews* 1:5 (December 1998/January 1999): 3.

"Demeter." *The New Review* 5 (1999): 42-45. Also appeared in *AveNews* 1:5 (December 1998/January 1999): 3.

"What a Wife Knows of Bones." *Confluence* 9 (1998): 63.

"Blue is a tongue in the snake of nature." *Troubadour* 2:1 (Fall/Winter 1998): 23.

"House Pleasures." *The New Review* 4 (1997): 107-108.